By the Way

Poems over the Years

By the Way

Poems over the Years

David Radavich

Buttonwood Press
Champaign, Illinois

1998

Buttonwood Press
P.O. Box 206
Champaign, IL 61824-0206

Book design by David Strange

Thanks to the editors and readers of the following magazines, in which some of the poems in this collection appeared previously: *Albany Review, Deus Loci, Elemental Poems I, Farmer's Market, First Intensity, Heidelberg Review, Journeyman, Orbis, Poet and Critic, Poetpourri, Tímarit Máls og Menninger, Time of Singing, The Times Literary Supplement, Treasure House,* and *Willow Review.*

Cover art: *Mountain Stream* by John Singer Sargent
   The Metropolitan Museum of Art, Purchase,
   Joseph Pulitzer Bequest, 1915. (15.142.2)
   Photograph ©1989 The Metropolitan Museum of Art

Publisher's Cataloging-in-Publication Data
Radavich, David
   By the way: poems over the years / David Radavich
      p.   cm.
   ISBN: 0-9658045-1-8 (hc)
   ISBN: 0-9658045-0-X (pbk)
   I. Title.
   97-72801 / 97-72323

First Edition

10   9   8   7   6   5   4   3   2   1

For Anne, whose lively, penetrating mind charms
and instructs all those around

Contents

I.

Arrivals

Refugee

He arrives at the Midwest
without a passport,
pulls up to the pump: Ellis Island
of the mind. Is this where
they check us in?
Puts back the nozzle,
plops down his VISA card, starts
signing the forms. Can't
remember the name they give him here.
Something flat, with corn
and soybeans in it.
They wonder why he wails
for the old country: Polkas, meat
lines, pickled pig's-feet,
clothes that smell like leeks.
No one wails here,
not even police wagons.
They clean life off with gasoline.

He pulls into the Midwest
looking at a boxcar rotting, half-open
as a hobo's eye, doesn't know
where these wheels will
take him, what's

next after the migration,
the sunflower, the prairie rat,
drying and wailing the noon-day sun.

Grecian Urn

My head in your hands
like a clay pot,
you in your thick Greek blur
trim my wayward hair,
tell me just what
to eat, the old country,
how your brothers come to eye
your thirty-year new life
checking over brides,
the girl you will send out
next month, I am invited, yes,
I am Orthodox, Russian—
"Cleveland not so bad, safe
in places where you go,
I pray never except
to be happy, don't worry, I
make you bee-yootiful,
you want the hair more thinner?
I make a good job, you see,
work hard, you make a good living"—
No, I don't smoke, sometimes
a little drink, not yet,
haven't found my bride, perhaps
in spring some year, I watch
the fat, yes, it's a nice city, heart
of a great furnace, yes,
I like my hair
glazed fine as urns.

You smile.

In an hour I know
Cleveland and Greece,
ripe goat cheese, marriage,
taxes, the hands
of a poet.

Installment

Our boxes never
seem quite
to fit our human lives.

They squeeze
and bend, overspill
into the air,

and yet
we carry
and stack
what souls
we have

far side of the porch,
and hope they bide.

Weary, our backs
curve down like weathered
vines beside the door.

That phone ringing
is only in our minds.

The neighbors don't know who
or what we bring, what
rooms we raise,

only the dog we follow

into the lamplight, leash
in tow, fraught
to the core, hungry,

tugging

the good way home.

Kansas Canticle

I.

She is a plain woman,
this hearty, encompassing Kansas.

No one could love her
who has not cursed the sun.

Her beauty is surplus
stripped to the grain, fruit
torn from the core.

Hair rolls out in freshly
parted rows, in seasoned curves
and eccentricities.

When she moves, it
is the gold of sheaves

casting glances.

Hers is a fertile breast
where truant whirlwinds play.

II.

Kansas is a room devoid
of ornament, known in the flat
of walls, in windows and floors.

Nowhere is left to hide
behind doctrine and the wildweed:
The orator answers himself.

Audience hills rustle

a sibilant, restless choir
beyond our basic conversations.

Against the sky, fields
of sunflowers in June vanity—

husky odor of rye, lame
adamant reflex of simplicity.

Barns and silos dot
the golden landscape like chairs

in a room, doors ajar,
sash-less windows
with wild-eyed draperies.

III.

One can die well in Kansas.

There's no conflict
in the anthem which departs
and the bare woodenness of flesh
laid out in chalky earth.

Crepe textures of skin,
at death, crinkle like August
grain, accept

the blush of nettles
on the cheek with nodding
anonymity. Here

the bare rhythms of a man
are stripped of the glorious

shroud and the munificent tomb:

The pyramids are not more reticent.

Bicycle Assembly

A distant, humble cry this is
from those heedless summer afternoons
brimming over the green billowing
hills in a mild clatter of rotating wind.

Wrench in hand, unrelenting, spoke,
pedal, and brake find their special orbits—
gradually, with some ellipsis
and odd thinking.

Buddha had it right:
Detach, know when something gets away,
when it spins down the road
with your brain clinging to dust.

Grab hold
of a new idea.

Ah, yes, this bolt
needs another good turn
and the right squeeze behind

to free ankles into

the circles of their being

Charleston, Illinois: Summer '94

Lincoln stalks here almost every day.
With his moral finger raised
in the air, towering over the prairie—
it's hard not to laugh, or cry.

Ears of restless corn ache
in the August heat, teenagers squeal
out of McDonald's, the Square
pulses leisurely,
winged with canopies.

Time stops again,
without an opinion.

The sky, blue like chicory,
limns the mind, the straight-arrow
road through the fields

that erupts into
grain silos, abandoned sheds,
Wal-Mart space stations,

a tilting old graveyard
lumpy under trees.

Everyone seems to drive by
in pick-ups with country tunes,
hard rock, blasting, baseball caps,
last plumbing job of the day,

courthouse chimes,

a few elders climbing into vans,
students clumped in bored disobedience.

It's history nobody sees,
busy with stoplights, errands.

Yet the air is thick
with the omens of sycamores

shivering in the wind,

the old log cabin '
twists its white smoke,

horses in the baked pastures
glance sideways, then move toward home.

Mercy

January-cold,
snow sits mounded
on the Colorado spruce
like a fat Buddha

glistening in sun

Nirvana
this must be

not to shiver
not to talk until spring

and then the tulips
sit bulbous

atop themselves
stems
of rebirth

I think of you digging
with cow manure

planting the colors
row upon row

that now hide
smug and whitened

under a winter moon

Meditating
now and here

O great white lie.

II.

A Season in Cancer

Preparation:
Thoughts before Surgery

Like a festive bird, I am
alive with feathers.

Every source, every appendage
has its own intonation.

All is in array.

I feel the air move across bones.

When they call my name,
an echo answers

from another tree.

For now there is no flight:
Only muttering of seed

and some clinging.

A song.

Some days are mad journeys,
clouds, colorations

that nature has built into the soul.

Skin-Head Blues

Being bald in December
is like wearing longjohns in July:

The world looks turned somehow inside out.

Just when everyone's warm
to the season,

donning antlers and mistletoe,
growing wool to fend off the freeze,

my skull-cap covers what
is not there:

Guarding the mad brain-cells left.

Not much given to revenge,
part of me wants to
skip naked in snow and call it

"Delusions in Grandeur"

Chiaroscuro

The trees don't know their own shapes.

That's for the winter sun
and the birds that sing there.

Those of us who pass by
in the frigid air

remark of skeletons and cobwebs,

how curious it is that sculptures
make their way into the world community.

But what of a tuft of hair,
that it can't be taken

away and the same bare head remain,
even in the direst of winters?

Things lose face in
time: Without effacing.

The squirrel's advice is that
this has not been a year of good seeds.

I think it's a matter of
making do with the fundament:

Be still about shadows;
let the sun speak loud.

In the Shell

Life has its weapons.

I've sharpened my claws so
I can just pluck

what barely sneaks across my path.

The blue sky: A new ring
to adorn my finger.

The clang of neighbors:
A new symphony I'll concoct
for my next soirée.

Back against death, in blanket,
I clutch my gift in the
breeze:

A self

so hard and so sure.

Valediction:
Forbidding Mourning

You've become my intimate.

I'm quite sure you have red hair
and quiver when you laugh.

Your freckles rap
each time
you greet me at the door.

You never call:
But how to

turn away that darkest relative?

Ours is a long, solemn,
meandering conversation with

no mock levity—

the kind between friends
who know the abandoned sorrow,

who chuckle together
over the shared cartoon.

We are able to sit together.

You are one who knows
my comings and my goings,

my thefts,

my everlasting dreams
of the bedchamber.

And I know your whereabouts.

Don't leave without first wiping
your shoes, send a picture
post card

from your new home

in the neighboring body.

III.

This World

Parkscape

I.

We come here to find
what is missing.

To seek the beguiling comfort
of trees, the absent
face, the color
lacking
our bright reveries.

We even drop a few barriers,
glance into the eyes of strangers—
but not too intently, not
with too much ease—
because it's the same need;
we don't wish to
acknowledge the likeness.

Instead, we circle
like egrets in search of a place
to rest our feet, to peer
into the dry, rippling water
and find sustenance
before we fly
outward in our perhaps
elegant aloneness.

It is dusk;
we have fed on it.

We know better than to stay too long.

A good park lets us fill
our emptiness with

dry breadcrumbs of passers-by.

II.

At day's end, a broad
sunset on a cooling bench,
laughter by the shore,
fog creeping over the skyline,
vague wink behind a speckled veil:

soothes what was fatigue,
the day's dark
madness

into sanity,
faint glittering
allure of autumn night

on the edge

of remission

Pride

We Americans ought
to erect a law

that it can't get
colder than minus twenty

or warmer
than ninety-five

in the winter
in the summer

outlaw all quakes
and hurricanes

the sudden
frost

curtail all clouds

Then punish Nature when
she disobeys,

spray all her crops

soil her streams

cut down her trees:

A bald woman is not so proud.

Persian Gulf Watch

Let crocuses come.

Let everything come,
dance before us like cabaret
or searing ghosts
in this mad, sad world.

Somewhere in clinics
heads twitch in their blisters,
eyes welded shut,
the accuracy of our minds
is called to question.

It's hardly real
what we see on TV, behind
the dots colored
as if they connected.

I look at my hand
like a bomb, searching
for life-lines,
more than guilty
of a few wild deeds.

This blanket of snow
is everywhere—
even on the screen
when the war has ended

for the night
and the colored dots take
refuge, pressing

hard against the ground,
screaming
spring, spring.

Thin Man: Bosnia, 1993

His legs, everywhere,
seem to reach out, extend, fold
back on him like a spider,

all arms and legs
and that one head helpless
in pain, in wakelessness

Someone claims
this is just, this is
history's remaking,

>whosoever does not
>believe
>must cry out

empty-boned in living flesh,
black spear-eyes
eating at the brain

Human insects
gathered
in a web of war

like flies that stuck
can not tear off
their wings.

Abe Lincoln on Donahue

You sit high in your unkempt beard
as if nothing had happened.
Not even a shudder.

I can't believe you're still
that ugly, no face-lift.
Phil's not quite sure what to say.

Here it is, our America,
sunk across the dusty globe,
come to our coins all scattered

like pain we worship,
this division without unity,
this violence addicted,

reality like a huge clutch of beads
with no string, all Nature flat
on her back, screaming.

Abe, this is serious.
How can you just sit there nodding?
This audience paid good money
for sweet answers.

Come on. Pick up the pieces.

Two Modern Nightmares

Or, Shipwrecked at the Mall

I.

I scan my wild, darting
eyes over the waves,
across the throbbing aisles,
my fingers rowing
with nervousness, pulling
myself nearer, nearer, imagining
everyone climbing after
merchandise
pretending to be saved,
mounting the battering tides,

blue light screaming
on the horizon:

Rescue is a tolling clerk
with a face that sometimes speaks.

II.

I run my sagging boat
along the shore,
up that narrowing spine
within the sands,
shivering, half-dead,
cursed by my nattering lust,
craving, scared to pay,
falling to land
in a lump,

I hear the sacred
mask intone:

Your card's expired!
Oh, you savages of the sea.

Listening to
Gregorian Chant

Time goes blank
five hundred, maybe seven
hundred years

on the edge

a new troubling
century

and that's a comfort
a strange comfort

Maybe the Dark
Ages weren't so dark

lighter
than our own

more believing
or more desperate

maybe they saw
the black and terrible

Infinite

We bury ourselves
forgetting:
                alcohol, crack,
scandal sheets, sex

We can't
meet ourselves

Face to Face

That voice within us
Longing

Chanting

Toe

It's easier
to focus

on the
small things

Not merely
the step forward

tiny index
of human

progress

moving
the upright

strangely

toward
the unknown

I can take you
in my hands

massage the sore
ravages

without knowing
where to go

a soft new way

even a stoneless
wandering,

this one among many

always tied
in fate

to the community
of nations

emigrating
one ridge, one vale

one bloody
siege at a time

We depend on
some forward some

bare
foundation

however small

E Pluribus Unum

It has been fused together,
our nation. After divided decades
we sit in front of the same
TV, cringe
at the same torture,
lurk in the same glittering
malls, crave together
what we can't
afford, gobble our food
in the same white
styrofoam,
dream together of
ultimate, violent sex:

To live the same
husk, same
purple blood, same
iconography of burning ash.

At last, at last.

IV.

Inundation Rhapsody

Inundation Rhapsody: Midwest 1993

St. Charles, West Alton, Davenport—
the names flood past
like the roofs of houses

arched and powerless

This is the reverse
of purification, cleansing,

everything filmed
in cisterns

After the quick, brandishing skies,
the slow creep up
the marooned wallboards

we watch
yet cannot see

Romance gives way
to railroad ties, barges,
débris, sandbags, cloacal flux,
trees stuck

like broccoli
in that muddy sauce

The ache of every bed, chair,
appliance, desk, books
that normally
frisk and run now

bound in place like
Antaeus, prisoner of the earth,
in water, anchoring water

This slow, lapping reaching
makes immobile even

the eyes
rapt, staring
dry as summer bone

Standing at the cliff's edge
secure in ideology

we confront: Passion

The Father of Rivers
makes us all children again,

asking for lessons,
begging for our place

to be sheltered,

being turned back
from the knee
to our own pain and path

Is there any other way
to know streamings of mind,

terrors that
spill out
visibly
in torrents above

below
crawlings
the pace of fear

clutching our ankles,
our own dragging demons?

Not just water
but all our obsessions

pour out,
take over the land:

Protect us, governments, God,
return us to our lives

without residue,

without anxiety, sludge,

the life we knew
we want
returned unscathed, insured

That crazy Rain Dance
must have worked its charm,

we were athirst
twirling like crazy,

searching for deliverance
from the dry days,

desert of our century's dying end

Mirages fired
the mind

I remember
when I saw you, mountains
of the southwest,

Mexico, blue and dry,
hazy in the heat
of distance,

long dry road as
far from here as Jupiter

How could life be otherwise
but an ark in pairs—

poems, parasols, plastic bottles,
all the paraphernalia

of ourselves
floating downstream
like a dream

before us

Our history floats by
awful in its diuretic honesty

Let us not forget
locality,
the individual human face
stolen into pain,

life's photographs
eroded and disfigured

Wrong bird
hiding out in the wrong nest,
wrong tree, even nature
is confused

O waters gathering
high and low

surrounding and imprisoning,

bring our leavings
right
before us,

century of greed
and waste

Carry out our baggage,
empty sins,

hubris
and despoilment

into

the Mouth of Life,

source of ends
beginnings
the wide claiming sea.

V.

Between Us

Gazelle

I've never seen one, glancing
at itself in a wide hollow, learning
the summer wind, bending
to sip in Africa—
but you raised your smooth
foot up graceful as a gazelle,
one poised above the other,
back arched against
the wall,
a crowded room.

If love is a gesture,
then let mind photograph:
You bent the room at your angle,
proficient geometer,
rubbed tendrils with a stone,
leaned your voice with a
single bud drooping.

You didn't
need to smile.

When you leave,
go away into the night
knowing your own delicacy,
    knowing your slim leg draped
is my staff
    in the dark vale.

Firefly

I don't mean to be
vulgar now, but when you
narrowed your still
thighs, it was
like a firefly lighting
the night just over the hill,
with its lantern along-
side a bush,
                    and I
came chasing, daunting
your wings with
the warm cup of hands
that were clapping gingerly.

Crossbred Driver

This catalogue
makes flowers look
like ladies
along the road.

Never could keep
posies straight
from peonies, azaleas
and rhododendrons,
autumn bulbs
purple and red.

Now they tell me
there's peony-lookin'
tulips, daffodils
like hyacinths that hang
all shy and lonesome.

It's just colors
made up at the factory,
pulled out of some
smelly darkroom
they paid a
pretty penny for.

Nothing that'd grow
in my little plot.

I remember pulling in
one night at a truck-stop,
tipped a pink waitress
five dollars
for a fifty-two
cent cup of coffee,

waited for her to blossom
in the parking lot,
sniffed long
at the wind, got in,
drove clear across Kansas
straight into the dark.

Serenade

My typewriter has
latent
tendencies

slides its scaly,
rippling flesh beneath
cold fingers

gets hot
and flustered

runs and chortles
its tight, dry pulse

chokes
and spits
glorious words

to me

when I am
awash and sorry

greedy

my typewriter
sings

and holds

my hands

Icicle

I would have taken you
in my hand, cold
as February sunrise,

tapered as a candle at dusk,
dripping and luminous
with all the frigid glamor

of a woman's kiss
before she goes inside
herself, into the vacant ground,

still thinking of that
moment hanging, being pulled
and willing in the air,

would have taken you
in my hand, firm
and fastened as a star,

but then you slid naked,
almost shattering
into unregions of the known.

On Marriage

Road is a metaphor
that comes to mind. But

that sounds altogether
too bumpy, one

thinks of mud-puddles
and sharp curves.

Metal bees.

Perhaps water, the sensation
of floating, feeling

gracefully untied yet
carried in one

direction—
only down, down to the
sea-bed where all mermaids lie.

Light perhaps, moving
in every direction, every
color, stable

and necessary—
when not benighted.

A walk in woods,
overhanging, undergrowing,
uncertain path and one

leaf cradling
another.

I would wish you
more than these: too many
metaphors to count,

a web of silk,
a line of waxen tulips
outside the door,

alien saucers
dropping occasional

surprise

before your feet:

Be magical in time.

Foot Massage

Your mouth curls up
like the keel
of a Viking ship
carving through fjords,

that lazy crust
of irony crinkling
to a smile:
My hands are explorers.

Telegraph wires
send direct
from heel to head,
dendrites talk electric,

ball bearings rotor
round the track,
squeal on
two fat tires.

Wild territory you
would book passage to
and sail beyond
the flat Old World.

Arch in my fingers,
your adulthood
collapses like clay
in a kindergarten class,

toes become plums,
I that boy
in the corner,
thumbs baking a pie.

No Excuse

Without this mindache
I would find

enough words

Legs flop
like broken wings

Kitchen walls
sag in yellow wallpaper

Light bulbs blink
too indisposed to hum

You sit expectant
not too proud

And I know a brain on fire,
on fire

burns for nothing

Arrangement

Petal that flares
as a trumpet, orange
and blaring

Organ pipe, straight
and tall, prim as a loft
in silence

You in my arms
being plucked in spring

Losing our roots
together

In water
atop a mahogany table

Our decoration

Ourselves
regarding each other

Instruments—
sacred and renewable—

I will help you
plant seeds.

Parting by Day

Glove is such a pauper image,
shaking its acquaintance.
Your hand fits my—what?—
life, yours against mine,
resting, alongside, inside, not
separable blue in a sky
not long huddled with clouds.

Speaking is a hardship
when the bleak sun screams
its innocence, fat evangelist,
alarm clock set to go off
in your eyes I see turn away
into nothing that is known, barren
soil that darkens and remains.

Go, take your separate journey
I feel as a pit inside, no engine
starts the way I stutter, go
with the wind, or like a snail
crawl into the forest, leave
your sticky trail, yes, lasting,
stuck, growing these great red leaves.

VI.

Kindred

Our Brood

The flower pots
would rain small crumbs
over the house,
the phone would ring
and we would race to hide,
rubbing between our gritty palms
a plot of six-year-olds:
Sly, stubby, mudtipped thumbs
clawing the ground
and pulling pants down
to throw dirt in;

against the summer oven
wind, in underwear
damp with play,
we leveled our naptime
pillows, dashed our dreams,
pulled our short
brown legs and rubbery
arms across the manicured corners
of the ghostsheet, kicking
culprits to the floor;

the snowy seasons
with gay charitable trees
we scurried by in knitted feet,
rode new bicycles,
overstuffed our cheeks
brown in kisses,
poured tea
from the doll-house,
scampered after
fluttering ribbons, papers, bows;

no classtime ever
in our minds, only hassocks
to throw, and frogs,
we would break
our gums
for the tooth-fairy,
clutch and toss pineapples,
blast marbles with our peanut toes,
plant prune-pits,
remembering the slooww
ring of the phone
when the sitter was gone,
dialing some phantom,
asking for chocolate shake,
and smearing dirt in our mouths.

Legacy

A friend of my father's,
when he was a boy,
dived off a bridge into
the Connecticut River
on a bewitching autumn day
when the breeze was
just cool from the east
and school was
a favored aversion—

dived and split open
his head
on a ledge just
under the surface.

I've often thought on
the spilling of that brain
into the water,

the horror
of boys looking

down without knowing
just what their wide eyes,

jagged swimming trunks
could do

about a fissure

in their very bones,
an indelible scar seared

into the recesses

of adulthood,

that shatters
even in the retelling

of a sunny blue day not far
from home.

Bounty

My father was never one to hunt.
Or find. Barely decked out in faded
dungarees and tattered shirt,
he'd let the stag run
wild in speckled beauty,
moving on himself, scattering
his eyes like seeds at early planting.

A snowy egret lit as much
in his forehead as on the willowed
narrow riverbanks and turned,
refreshed, to take up further sustenance.

A stick myself, I'd run behind
and fail to see more than two antlers
getting the best of us, shouting,
"Aim, Dad!" and no more.

Now I hold the rusted knife
before me, having lost my share
of points, about to seize
the raw inside and pluck it out,
blood upon blood, muscle,
everlasting bone.

Here it is, Dad; warm in the hands.

Prayer for My Mother

Ever since I saw your face
streaking through rye-fields,
propped in sleep against
the cold glass of a German train,
still and emotionless,

I've known you could die.

After all those
seasons and furrows,

such violent watersheds,

who would have thought the prairie
grass could leave the prairie?

But here you are laid out,
flattened of the
very life you brought.

Yes,

there are words
and opportune deities,

and rows of cellophaned flowers—

but you are an entity
without prior arrangement.

Even now
you are luminous.

I wish you a rise into the morning,
with your crisp brightness

greeting the sun.

February Mask

The dead seem more awake
than the living

in this crisp snowy façade
that covers the season's gaiety

in a death-mask we
call winter

But it's just
springtime lurking—

in every season another hides
urging its seed, laboring its sap—

one day we will throw off
this all-weather, sagging flesh,
pull out these cloudy eyes
that fail to see,

unlock the breast-plates of desire,
give wisdom another chance
in someone else's young façade

in the darkness lurking

And you, my daughter,
whose seasons whirl still
like a carousel,
won't hide your gaiety

as I wake to
a more dying flesh:

Sing out the new hymn
that has risen
to be born in you;

unfold us to the world again
as only a child can
wake a parent

whose snows
hide a multitude of stars

In Memoriam

The old Dodge Dart, aged '74, creamy
and tattered in places, driving
55 on the Interstate, proud in that right lane,
defiant yet soft and pliant
to my hands and eyes, rumbles
one cylinder short toward
its new classy home:
behind the Subaru showroom.

It's not abandonment, really.
Not quite. It's putting to pasture,
hoping there's heaven somewhere
for good, reliable (if stodgy) cars,
motors with quirks, curses, personalities

That take on time-dispelling colors
of family quarrels in the back seat, trips
mistakenly taken, sacred dents telling all now
in some country junkyard.

Sleeping, I suppose.
Gossiping about the good old days.
Telling layered narratives with
inset stories within inset stories
and abrupt tense shifts
without proper transitions.

Definitely in need of some editing.

But one prefers to think the old war-horse
has begun a new clandestine, torrid existence:
beneath the hands of a mad teenager, hair
long and the tightest jeans that can
plot the tangled routes of young arteries.

Racing around, scared out of its wits
and just ahead of the local police.

It's only life. We all die and go
to heaven (don't we?), where we finally
get a new cruise control and power
locks, retractable antenna, everything
comfortable, adjustable to fit that sagging
old age that longs for the fit of the

First jeans in the first car,
cruising, picking up life
and knowing, by damn,
this is a racy, bucket-seat world

That lasts as long as the next
big thrill, and then some.

Rest in peace.

Man with the Snow-Blower

The time is now. Snow falls gently,
and the neighbors' motors rev
up, the back remembers
lifting all that white weight
last year, somewhere he read that more
heart attacks occur in front
of the garage than anywhere else.

Better to be safe. Sooner or later,
everyone ends up at Wal-Mart.

He pulls the cord and marvels
at the spumes of snow lifting, lifting
over the driveway edge shivering
opaquely somewhere under a
frieze of heavy, wet preponderance.

This would have killed his back
last year. He would have yelled curses
at his wife, made her brew tea (spiked to ease
the pain), and clutched at his chest—
partly for sympathy, partly
to atone for boyish foolhardiness

believing he could shovel with
the best of them, gung-ho and wise,
imagining himself somewhere
new on the frontier
a century or more ago.

It's harder than it used to be
by hand, getting the margins right.
A snow-blower makes him feel old, somewhat
silly, a perfectionist in snow,
sculpting his mounds like blessings.

Most of the neighbors still drone.
Soon silence will descend,
and the precise order of every
lawn will glisten in the domed white

only the man with the motor
could ever wish for, or attain.

The Twenty-Year Poem

(For John Guzlowski)

The man
has been writing
his poem for twenty years.

His child
is grown up now,
has gone to college,
chosen an antithetical career,
given birth to monsters.

His wife divorced,
he sits alone
puzzled but content
beside an artificial fire
that nonetheless
warms and saddens him.

Those wild contractions
he wielded formerly
like a demon
now creak
under the hump
of years.

And still he knows
this oracle
will never be as fine
as his forty-year poem, begun

long since, that smolders
unfinished in the bureau drawer
next to the sixty-year
poem, which is

73

potentially
the glory of all

anyday

emerging
from revision

curling out
its white smoke

announcing

At last,
the new Poet

is chosen.

VII.

Egyptian Days

Swimming Near El-Alamein*

This bluest green water
eyes have ever seen, shimmering
against whitest sand

soft as seashells melted
to carpets of pearl—

massages each toe,
each leg, each strand of hair.

No time is enough
to linger

in this world

no body
too old, too worn,
too ulcerous.

These arms spread wide,
these eyes, sun takes its bow,

voices of strangers,
children, sudden friends
laugh

each wave home

too fast

I see your face
calling with a towel,

welcome, offer of cigarettes,
and the best day's end

hosting the return

we don't want
we never want

what the world calls us to

dark labyrinths
of fate

Our pain has flown,
let it stay on the wing:

wide over the jeweling sea

its shield of gold

*A World War II battle site marked by a museum and three
international cemeteries

Monastery at
Wadi Natrun

How to make sense
of need?—

Christians in a Muslim
land, disciples of St. Mark,

the Alexandrine
visitor,

these herds of camels
loping, sand pastures, wind-
blown shrubs and

then

these crosses,
multiplying in rows

as necklaces,

breast upon sanded breast
with slitted eyes,

dry hollow passages

through time

This is the desert
beyond words.

God rounded to chapels
in punishing sun,

wind flailing
the brazen flame trees

and this horde
of humans

touching the sacred
relic, summoning strength

from bone necessity

a life in sand

that stays and stays

The cleric robes
hang loosely, simply
in the heat, move graciously

as naked feet begin

to pray.

Catacombs at
Kom el Shogafa

Down and down
this cylinder winds,

necropolis of cultures

into the earth,

Pharaonic, Ptolemaic,
Roman images superimposed,

wearing each other's
inscriptions,
faces, clothing—

one must be safe
about the underworld,

respect all gods

adorn all sarcophagi

remember where life goes
and stays

We bend our necks,
crane and weasel our way
along this deepest

memory

dialogue of history,
human ingenuity

to face
the other life

in rock, with swords
and sheaves

May the journey
be peaceful, fulfilling:

the gods of time

safely

engraved

beside us

Cavafy's House

The face, I think.

Lingers from a high house
above this balcony

overlooking

the laundry
of everyday life.

Ignorant of the words
that emanated

from this
marbled face

amid the tattered books
of a life, a being

in rooms
in ancient songs,

these multitudes
come and go

in their daily worn bodies

like rhyming ghosts

A beggar asks
a fee,

stands to profit
the memory of a poet

who lived
who lives

sequestered

beyond a street
that offers cameras,
leather, jewels, the rugs

of nomads,

who traveled farther
than all these

naming

heroes in air.

Visiting an
Alexandrine Mosque

We leave our shoes,
tiptoe over rugs in silence,
wife among women,
myself among reclining
men who read or sleep or
think or merely be.

It's cavernous, this dome,
and fully carved, the chandelier
must weigh some tons.

Some thousand marvels
yet this ease, this hanging
around in time

eye of the city
calm
unblinking

a faceted jewel

to circumflect inside

It's hard to put on
shoes again

this treading to busy streets,
vendors and vended,

horns shrieking

this calm to veiling
memory

Along the Nile

This could be the Mississippi,
the Ohio, the Missouri,

but the mind
knows better—

palm trees, mansions
on either side, gleaming
mosque at the crook
of the current,

Cleopatra somewhere
glittering on her barge—

it's a lesson in
recognition and return.

We have been
in this small wooden
hand-hewn skiff

puttering by ourselves

since childhood,

collecting shells
at the mouth
where waves right-angle
before our eyes

lunching under
grass-roofed tables

patrolling along
the limestone ramparts—

We have been
crafting these waters
for years,

papyrus growing
and being harvested

orange trees and
frangipani

workmen painting
their great wood boats—

We know in a wind
where we are.

VIII.

Departures

Flying

How little we see out
the windows of our lives.

The broad view, not the details,
the rivets on the wings, not

the wings themselves,
not forward, craning, askew

and the wind merely
hypothetical

over prairie dogs,
cacti, a wide yellow western

sky and all that sunset happening
just out of reach, friends

reading articles
to improve themselves

but not really flying, not seeing
the broken faces on the ground

trod in poverty and war
beneath our feet,

love hiding from us
never quite removing her glove,

nature sitting all too
grand, a stiff grandmother

whose limpid eyes
we dare not ask to keep—

Our landing is a jolt,
a bottom we get to without

being there.

Reading the Poet

I think somehow
you must be a passerine

who can move inside me
intimately, flapping your wings

To know about war,
its cries and whispers,

droning flares and the quick
spasm behind the bush

creating dead memories
that will never give birth

To learn loneliness
is not alone,

a cell gathering
its ravenous mitochondria,

sorting its belongings
for a journey, a long journey

To sense that love
copulates in the mind, spreads

lily pads on calm waters,
shoots down anchor

that the blossoms claim
carefully, only before friends

To fly with your wings
somewhere in a gusting wind,
a sudden firm foundation
heading north south

away from

this broken body.

Jack's Funeral

A man of sturdy stock,
he smoked himself to this.

December wind rattling
through grass,

bare hills brown
with possibilities and no more.

The green tent shudders
without thinking.

The minister's words, well-meaning,
droning, fail to warm.

Our eyes wander from book
to hole to faces to earth to sky.

Slowly, behind our backs
a herd of deer,

fifteen or twenty at least,
chase their leader

dust of the air
in a cimarron wake

fence after fence

the tall grass

beyond the western horizon

Widow's Weeds

Every time the wind-chimes
wrangle in the storm
outside
above the patio,
she sees again his dying
form: white as the bed-sheet,
churning, sometimes
clutching,

sometimes staring
like a sphynx with forefeet
in the swirling sand.

It's a vision that tolls
and tolls, even in the poems
she now writes

aching that answer,
trying to discern a tune
or even a face
she can live with

in the blank
mirror of her days

The dress she lives
in doesn't even drape
an open leg.

Mornings
sit and
hardly move.

Give her a soft
warm drink.

Echoes vaguely
in the wind, stuttering.

Uncle Jerry's Words to the Wise

First off, believe
what you don't hear.

Adults won't tell you
what gives them chills:
They don't want
you stealing it.

Read between the lines,
like with deodorant ads.

That stuff doesn't
conjure up women!

And believe, a girl's
hem is not what's exciting.
(Can't speak for boys' butts.)

You wanna die?
So do most of us Mondays.

You just lost your monopoly on pain.

Being loved? That's a cinch.
Give somebody worse
off than you a folded rose.

Take to the streets when
you grow up

When the night's all
silent, tight with itself,
insidious with content

Take to screaming
your name

Ceremonies in Time and Space

A night sky. The dark fields
recumbent yet alert.
Jupiter glistens in the constellation
Sagittarius: Hope for a new age.

Overhead, unseen,
a space station orbits connected
by computers, broadcasts,
two former enemies
locked together
coupling, de-coupling
now like first-time lovers,
strange, not awkward,
somehow natural,
to be hoped for again

Elsewhere the riots continue,
bombings, and the hatred
of another face,
another body unlike
our own, blood and last

breath on every city
and neighborhood visited
day and night
without rest
around
the visible globe

The overhead lovers,
exuberant, exhausted, converted
to a new faith, new rite
in the summer
atmosphere, feel

surprised
when the visible triumphs
over the invisible

The stars in the night,
far away, puncture
the darkness.

Birthday

Every year a leaf falls,
one at a time, hands,
days full of raking, scattering

and I come to see
the bare tree
of us
against the sunlight
strewn in branches, shimmering
naked against all

those colors
you give me tumbling
free within
a small space, a time together

walking in woods

Refracting

One's mind keeps
returning to spiders

Their busy legs
working, spinning the spun
universe

Refracting
the sun's hued prism

Every corner
tree, brick, face

Whatever stands still
long enough to be

Caught

The ultimate
maker

Pulling hard into
the integumented dance

Making

What
never stops

Until the dark hand
parts the web

Burying the Dead

One ought to remember the dead.
Even the dead we never knew,
the sourceless beings
we carom against in weed-studded life.

The homeless man we gave
a ride home from church, gasping
his near-last breath,
to a pharmacy bench outside
that last infallible air-conditioning.

A woman with cancerous breast,
next-door neighbor, teacher, friend,
her mammoth frazzled husband
carrying her brave
knickknacks and Boston ferns
to prop them in a U-Haul
driving across a hopeless flatland.

The prairie grasses shiver,
remind us of fecundity.
I do not know how
to cry, or to bury.

From a distance all blue
chicory looks alike, cool frame
for a hot, hot road leaving

all manner of corpses
under our wheels.

Sea-Canticle

That old companion washes the sand,
its cadence of life lapping our feet,
tugging, tossing, rearranging.

Year by year a few of us
disappear, sunk into the vortex,

shells drop and ache at sea-bottom.

Someone has eaten the insides
long ago, we continue as something else,

transformed, life's great beads
strung on a wave.

Looking out, you and I see scarcely
a ripple—artificial calm

even the sharks don't penetrate.

Wildness will take place
another time.
          This is a life
red when it awakens.

Let the shore sink and ooze
beneath our feet;

The moon rises to its new white face.